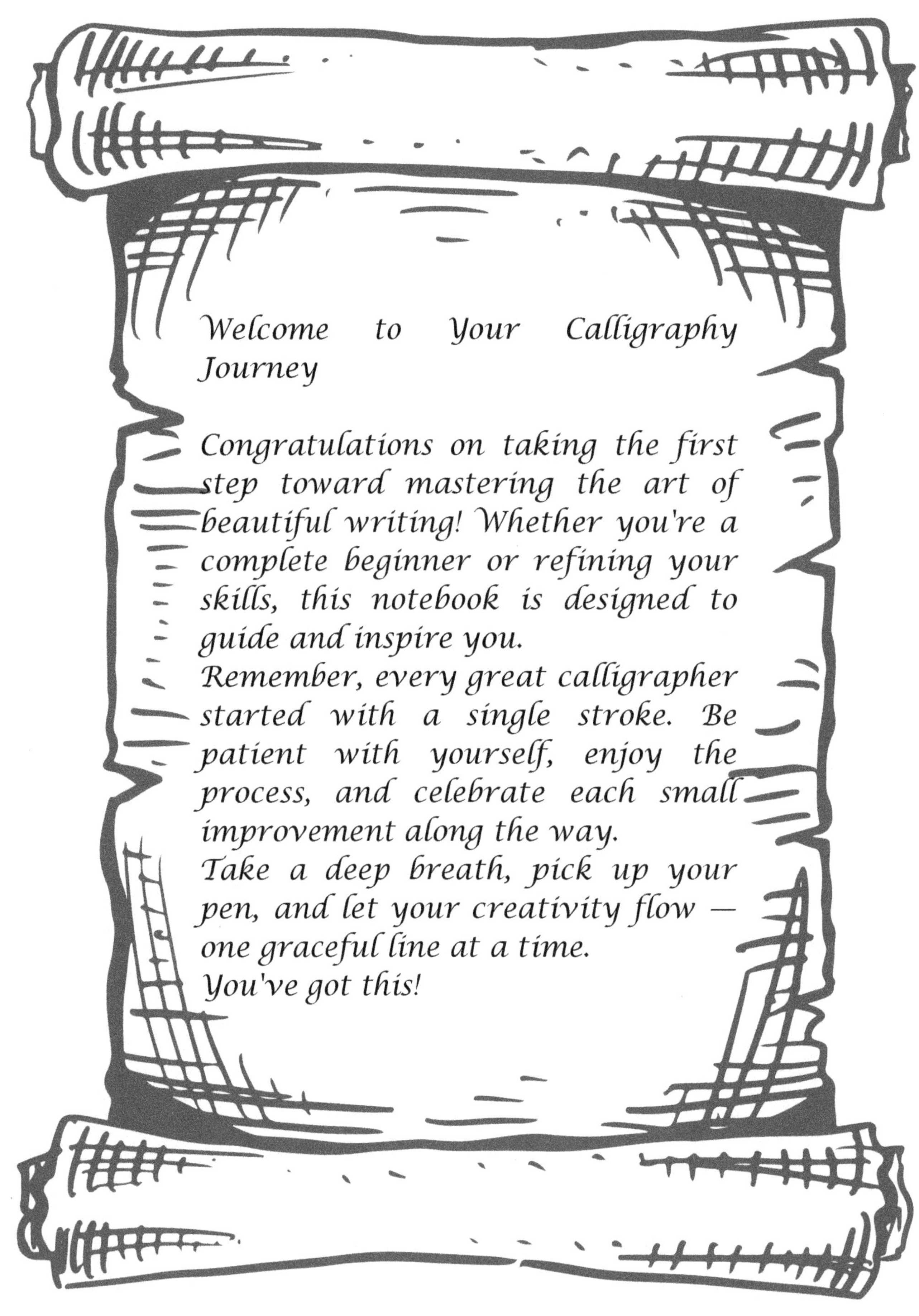

Welcome to Your Calligraphy Journey

Congratulations on taking the first step toward mastering the art of beautiful writing! Whether you're a complete beginner or refining your skills, this notebook is designed to guide and inspire you.
Remember, every great calligrapher started with a single stroke. Be patient with yourself, enjoy the process, and celebrate each small improvement along the way.
Take a deep breath, pick up your pen, and let your creativity flow — one graceful line at a time.
You've got this!

Amazing Calligraphy

This Book Belongs To:

____

Introduction to Calligraphy: A Beginner's Guide

Mastering the art of calligraphy is an enjoyable journey that requires patience, practice, and the right techniques. Follow these simple tips to improve your handwriting and develop elegant, flowing letters.

1. Proper Posture and Hand Position
Sit comfortably with your feet flat on the floor and your back straight.
Position your paper at a slight angle (about 45 degrees) to align with your natural writing motion.
Hold your pen at a 45-degree angle to the paper, applying gentle but consistent pressure.
Rest your arm lightly on the table and allow your fingers to guide the pen's movement.

2. Master Basic Strokes Before forming letters, practice these essential strokes:
Upstrokes: Light, thin lines created with minimal pressure.
Downstrokes: Heavier, thicker lines made with more pressure.
Ovals: Circular strokes that improve control and symmetry.
Curves and Loops: Useful for connecting letters smoothly.

3. Focus on Letter Formation

Start by practicing individual letters using guides or tracing sheets.
Pay attention to letter height, spacing, and proportions.
Repeat each letter several times to develop consistency.

4. Develop a Rhythm

Writing slowly and deliberately at first will improve your precision.
Gradually increase your speed while maintaining accuracy and flow.

5. Choose the Right Tools

Beginners may find brush pens, felt-tip pens, or calligraphy markers easier to control.
Experiment with different nib sizes and ink types to find what suits you best.

Practice Phrases for Calligraphy Exercises:

1. *The quick brown fox jumps over the lazy dog.*
2. *Success is the sum of small efforts repeated daily.*
3. *Practice makes progress, not perfection.*
4. *Creativity takes courage.*
5. *Dream big, work hard, stay humble.*
6. *Kind words cost nothing but mean everything.*
7. *Great things never come from comfort zones.*
8. *Believe you can, and you're halfway there.*

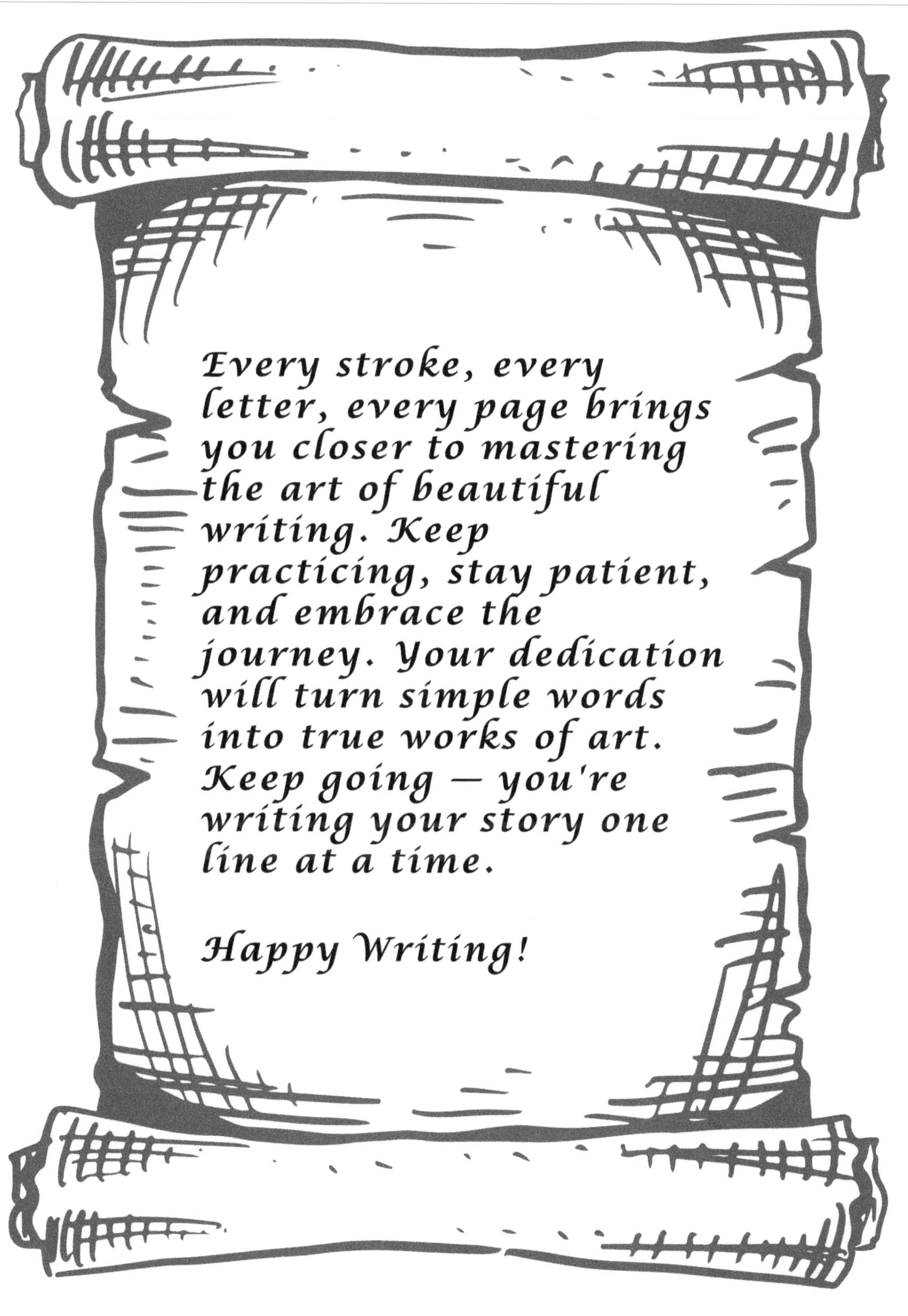

Every stroke, every letter, every page brings you closer to mastering the art of beautiful writing. Keep practicing, stay patient, and embrace the journey. Your dedication will turn simple words into true works of art. Keep going — you're writing your story one line at a time.

Happy Writing!

THANK YOU!

If you enjoyed this book and found it a source of joy for you, I invite you to leave a review on Amazon. Your words are eagerly awaited, they support me in what I create and give me the strength to continue with enthusiasm and passion!

With appreciation and gratitude,
Riya Edwards

We would really appreciate your feedback, please send us a email to:

ritirra@gmail.com